Reflections
on Life
in the
San Juan Islands

Reflections

on **Life** in the

San Juan Islands

by Mary Kalbert

Dream Lake Publishing
Friday Harbor, WA

Reflections on Life in the San Juan Islands
Copyright © 2009 by Mary Kalbert

Dream Lake Publishing
Friday Harbor, Washington

Cover photograph by John Miller
Section images by John Miller
Cover and book design by Pam Herber
Author photograph by Pam Herber

Library of Congress Control Number: 2009902958

ISBN: 978-0-9824282-0-7
          0-9824282-0-0

Printed in U.S.A.
First Edition

To my husband John
with love

Contents

Acknowledgements

A thank you to Jack Cory for allowing me to write for Island Guardian.com and suggesting I compile my columns into a book.

A special thanks to John Miller for his superb cover photograph of swans on our lake and the seasonal artwork included in the body of the book.

As always, a separate thanks to Alice B. Acheson for practical advice.

For work above and beyond, sincere appreciation to Pam Herber for cover design, text and content design, editing, general and specific advice, and for being a willing participant in this process.

Lastly, a thank you to my husband John for his abiding love and endless patience.

x

Introduction

There is a particular question asked of every islander who wasn't born here. It may come early in a budding friendship, or much later, but at some time the question "How did you get to San Juan Island?" will arise.

Our road to San Juan Island started in 1957 in Garden City, New York.

In 1957 my husband's parents welcomed Hartmut, a young German boy, into their home. He was participating in a year long American Field Service (AFS) program. The exchange, as we who participate in such exchanges say, "took."

In the decades that followed, college, careers, marriages and children kept our extended family together on both sides of the Atlantic. In 1994, Hartmut's youngest daughter asked to live with us in Oklahoma as an exchange student. We were elated with the possibility of a second generation exchange.

The request came to fruition through the Rotary Youth Exchange Program. At the end of Corinna's time with us, we asked her if there was something specific she wanted to see before returning to Germany. "Yes," she said without hesitation. "I'd like to see Orca whales."

We called long-time friends in Seattle who told us that the San Juan Islands should be our destination if we wanted to see the whales. We arrived in Friday Harbor on the Saturday of Memorial Day weekend of 1994. The ferry ride alone from Anacortes was worth the trip. The weather was rainy, foggy and cold. We loved it.

We dropped our bags at a motel on Spring Street and met with Captain Rick, owner of the Bon Accord, for a whale watching tour. Corinna and I opted to sit out on the foredeck in the rain to smell the salt water and scan the horizon. Near Lime Kiln lighthouse, we saw our first pod of whales. In the course of a half hour, one rose from the water in what I later learned was a spyhop. Another exploded in a—you-can't-top-this!—breach. Corinna was ecstatic. But I felt something stirring, a deeper yearning, something in that moment I could not articulate.

After our four hour trip around the island, we chugged into the slip at Friday Harbor. We walked slowly along the docks toward Spring Street. A pool of light from the Ale House invited us inside. We sat in a corner, had Shepherd's pie and quaffed pints of good Eichenberger Hefe-Weizen beer. Warmed and dry, we strolled up and down the streets and alleyways, wandered into small shops and watched the ferry silently arrive and leave again.

Armed with a map, we drove all over the island, to Cattle Point, South Beach, False Bay and Whale Watch Park. We stopped on Mitchell Bay Road to watch a fawn prance and nibble, stopped again to laugh at four wild turkeys gobbling to each other. On Roche Harbor Road, we stopped along the road at the Duck Soup Inn sign. We looked across the glistening pond, through the fog to the squares of yellow light glowing in the restaurant windows. From my passenger side window, a wooded island sat in the middle of a lake, shrouded in the same gray fog. An old white dinghy lay face down on a small dock.

"Can you imagine living here?" John asked me in a quiet voice.

"No." I didn't dare.

We discovered that each of us had felt "taken" with the island, an unspoken sense of homecoming we could not explain.

On a recent trip to Germany, we spent time with our friends. Smiling, Corinna asked us if we still felt the same way about island living.

Yes, we told her. Ten times over.

Winter

Winter

A Slow Waltz in Winter

With the holidays now but dim lights in the rear view mirror of my memory I look forward with quiet contemplation to the stillness of the gray and white days ahead, the smell of wood smoke from our chimney, the crackle and dance of flames in the kitchen fireplace, and steam rising from a copper pot of soup as it bubbles on the back burner of my old stove.

It is now that the Trumpeter swans, Canada geese and assorted duck families verbally vie for water around our dock. Who gets the biggest circle of unfrozen water in the lake and for exactly how long? These raucous arguments go on far into the night. Somehow they make their peace for when the morning fog lifts they are still there—quiet, resting, agreeable.

In this season when Mother Nature drapes us in her favorite wrap, our resident curmudgeons, with hats pulled low and collars high, step out of their frowns and chat with those of us who have remained throughout the winter. Will the snow be horizontal or vertical? Could be either. Will the wind pummel us today, or tomorrow? Could be both.

There is an unnamed ebb and flow among those who do not scatter to warmer climes. We engage in simple conversations about the wonder of a purple-hued sunrise, a child's school success, or a popular line from the community theater's latest production. We share pot-luck meals and recipes at club socials, hike along the roads devoid of bicycles and mopeds, and appreciate the slower pace of life that winter brings. On driftwood covered beaches we stroll, taking note of the rhythm of our lives in moments of welcome solitude.

This is the time for a slow dance with Mother Nature. After a high kicking spring, a fox trotting summer and a languorous tango through autumn, she's entitled to be a bit weary. For those of us who have stayed throughout the winter, we welcome the chance to slow waltz with the stately lady in the winter white robe.

Early Shift

It's raining. The wind howls down the chimney like a hungry cat. The last of the patio furniture just blew by on its way to Haro Strait and I don't care. I love the bluster and the smell, the unpredictability of fronts barreling in from the Pacific in a mid-winter welcome.

My nose comes out of our warm nest-of-a-bed followed by eyes that focus on the double skylights above us. I hear the splatter of big drops and a tree branch scraping the roof.

I slip out of bed, rooting around for my warmest pair of socks. In the closet, a favorite wool sweater has muscled its way to the top of the clothes stack.

Careful not to wake John, I pad to the kitchen and flip the switch on the coffee pot. The stray cat that arrived days ago to take up residence on my back porch has mewed his way into the mud room. He yowls in a modulated voice and pushes against the glass paneled door between the mudroom and the kitchen. "You're still on probation," I remind him as I open the door, turn on the laptop and reach for the cat food.

The computer hums and the coffee pot gurgles a puff of steam into the air. I feed the cat, lift my nose to catch the first scent of coffee and step outside. The swans in our cove loudly vocalize their plans, with complete disregard for the still sleeping ducks that dot the shoreline. The rain falls in bursts on the tile roof, and the wind whips my robe around my legs. I shiver for a moment in the stinging cold.

Back inside, with a Montana size cup of coffee, a blanket on my lap and my feet propped on the hearth, I call the cat. He peers around the island and gives his tail a lazy flick.

"Get over here before I get busy," I say. He ignores me.

"Look, I know this has to be your idea. So, I don't really want you up here." I adjust myself in the rocking chair. "I'm just going to hold this soft blanket. Go on, skedaddle."

He hesitates, then ripples toward me and in one graceful leap lands mid-lap. He showcases his back-side, a subtle reminder of who is really in charge, then turns and gently paws my shoulder. I am allowed to rub his head.

I sip. He purrs. I rub. He purrs. Daylight makes an entrance.

It will be possible to grow accustomed to this black and white purring heat pump. Two years ago our old cat, Last Chance, affectionately called L.C., died after eighteen years in our family. We have mourned his passing, but it may be time to consider another pet.

I sit until my leg stiffens and begins to tingle, and then move slightly to accommodate this cat's dead weight. "Dogs have masters," I mutter.

His emerald eyes narrow and he stares at me intently. I sense he is taking command.

"I know, I know. Cats have staff."

The Reciprocity Thing

We've had a long cold spell. A foot of snow has fallen and a partial thawing and a re-freeze have left us without electricity. Our long driveway is impassable.

"Look." John holds out his gloved hand. Iridescent green, with a speck of red on his crown, a tiny bird lays frozen in his palm. "Found him near the garage."

I don't recognize this miniscule thing. A quick look in our Audubon book tells me it is a Ruby-Crowned Kinglet. The olive wings and red on his crown patch identify it as a male.

I turn him delicately. "The description doesn't do it justice." In the pale sunlight his wings have a shimmer, his chest is a puff of pale green, and his eyes are ringed in white. Two white wing bars accentuate this feathered work of art.

"A casualty of winter." I look around at the tracks of deer and raccoon. "It won't be the last."

Winters here have taught us to be prepared. An old propane range has served us well. The trees that were felled by the wind in prior storms are stacked in firewood length on our porch, and our water supply is ample.

John stomps snow off his boots and smiles at me. "We'll

get the generator going and we'll be fine."

I look again at the tiny bird. Not everything is fine. I reach for the phone and call our neighbors, Jack and Heidi. "Need anything?"

Jack doesn't hesitate. "Yes, got some frozen pipes. Need a propane nozzle."

I relay the message to John who has the needed piece of equipment and a moment later is on his way across our acreage to lend a hand.

Island reciprocity is the oil that keeps life on this "rock" going. Heidi is the proud owner of a brood of happy hens. Throughout the year, in exchange for a bucket of grass clippings or the occasional bag of seasonal crab we have caught, I am welcome to sit and cluck with the chickens or gather eggs for my own use.

Not so long ago, another friend, Colleen, delivered fresh lamb to my door. A vegetarian, she is happy to raise lambs for the consumption of local meat lovers. In turn, I buy all the plants and shrubs I can from her nursery.

After a few minutes, the bread I had taken from the freezer earlier this morning has thawed. I slip on my boots and crunch my way carefully to a sheltered spot on the patio, tossing crumbs as I go. In exchange for food, the winter birds flit about and add vibrant color to the winter grayness in our lives.

Regretfully, I can do nothing for the Ruby-Crowned Kinglet, but I *can* strengthen the cycle of reciprocity that tightens the stitches in the fabric of island life.

Spelling Bee

In the heart of our winters, island living becomes a haven for all things community. Service clubs square off against students in our annual Knowledge Bowl. Under the direction of venerable Fred Yokkers, the high school theater production plays to packed houses. Book and poetry readings abound and island playwrights have a chance to see their works on stage. At the high school, the gym is packed with hoarse and sweaty Wolverine basketball fans, and track athletes pound along the roads in winter training. Talent of any ilk is recognized and applauded.

One such event happened last week as the Rotary Club of San Juan Island sponsored the third annual Friday Harbor Community Spelling Bee, held at the San Juan Community Theatre Main Stage.

Twenty-six entrants from Friday Harbor Elementary School, Friday Harbor Middle School, Spring Street International School and Paideia Classical School participated in the event.

First Place Winner was Michael Barsamian, a seventh grader from Friday Harbor Middle School. As a result of the win, his school was awarded $300, his classroom $150 and he personally received $75.

The finalist was Fiona Small, a fifth grader at Friday Harbor Elementary School. Her school was awarded $200, her classroom $100 and she personally won $50.

I had planned to be a part of the ever-growing audience but was volunteered by another volunteer to take some photos. It took a few seconds for me to see what a unique perspective I had. From my perch on the stage wing, I observed the audience and the spellers and I noted the following:

All the contestants listened intently, leaning forward in their chairs as Rotary President Jack McKenna explained the rules and noted which rules had changed since last year. As the spelling bee began, each student listened to the selected word, and some mouthed the spelling to themselves. They watched the other participants make their way to center stage.

Each contestant approached the pool of light, stood bravely in front of the microphone, peered into the blackness beyond and delivered vowels and consonants in the order their memory served them. A look at the judges for a green card sent some of them, with a sigh of relief, back to their chairs for another chance at the title. A red card signaled to others they were out of contention and sent them down the steps to a rousing round of applause for their effort.

The event that afternoon wasn't just a spelling bee. It was so much more than a youngster spelling a word. Courage and risk accompanied each child to the center of the spotlight, and grace and sportsmanship were at their side as they exited the stage. Admiration and pride spilled into the aisles from the friends and families that gathered there. Hugs had to form a waiting line.

Perhaps these children are yet too young to know that the life skills honed in a blinding circle of light before a too-tall microphone are a foundation that will prepare them for their lives ahead. But, I am not.

Kudos to them all.

Winter

Nor'easter Blow

"Whoa, did you hear that?" I turn to John as a gust of wind shrieks down the chimney of the fireplace in our bedroom.

"I don't think I want to get up just yet." He burrows under the covers.

Years of living in Oklahoma, the heart of Tornado Alley, have given me a special appreciation for the furious displays of Mother Nature. "I've got to see what's going on out there."

Our home sits in a sheltered spot inland. When we get high winds, we know that somewhere the island's edge is getting battered. I throw on some clothes and venture onto the patio where in a far corner pine limbs play their own version of Twister. At the woodpile the tarp on the log splitter has taken wing and wrapped itself around a tree in a lover's embrace. Lake waves slap against the dock and the morning birds are silent.

On my way back into the house the screen door blows out of my grip. Shivering, I turn the coffee pot on and search for my high-wind-and-cold-rain boots.

John wanders into the kitchen but isn't yet awake.

"I want to go to the beach." I find the boots and set them

on the kitchen hearth.

"What?"

"I want to go to the beach or down to Cattle Point." I realize the timing of my request is particularly poor, but the wind doesn't always hang around for folks to have oatmeal and juice.

"Why?" John is nothing if not logical.

"To get a picture." Sometimes I have to spell it out.

"Of?" He actually waits for me to answer that.

"I want to take my camera to the shoreline and take a picture of the water crashing against the rocks, or on the beach."

He pours oatmeal into his bowl and juice into his glass. "Oh."

I have obviously not made my case. What can I do here? A carrot. That is it. He needs a carrot.

"I'll help you pick up the limbs all the way to the mailbox." This is no small thing. Our lane is 900 winding feet of trees. Of course, I could just go out on my own. I would hate to see a spectacular sight without him, and truthfully, the fact he can drive our old truck in any weather might be a part of it too.

He peels a banana. "After breakfast."

That is a two word sentence. Things are looking up for me.

True to his word, after breakfast we bundle up and head out. Through the foggy window I see tree branches that have flung themselves across the drive in wild abandonment. It will take a lot of time to help them back into the woods.

At Jackson Beach, John maneuvers the old truck exactly into the position I ask. I open the door carefully and slide out into the shrieking wind. With my camera in hand, I inch forward, leaning against the truck. I lift my head as a gust of wind roars over the truck and slaps my camera up into my face. It blows my hands around until I hit myself in the face a second time. In general, it has its way with me. I fetal-position myself against the wheel well to catch my breath.

The wind tugs my prized possum-down hat I bought in New Zealand in the direction of freedom. I smash it further down onto my head and manage to hold the camera still for one pathetic photograph.

A friend drives by and rolls his window down. He yells that he wants a copy of anything good that I get.

"Fat chance," I snort, ducking into waves of stinging rain.

I scramble back to the door of the truck, fling it open and tumble onto the seat. "Enough of this." I touch my cheek just under my eye. "I think I have a shiner."

"What's next?" John has given me what I have asked for and is patiently waiting.

"Take me home." I slump down into my coat. "Some weather is best experienced from the safety and comfort of your own nest."

Winter

Yufka Days

This past Saturday I spent the afternoon with Gretchen Allison, Chef and Owner of Duck Soup Inn. Along with eight eager people, I participated in Gretchen's hands-on cooking class—this one being "The flavors of Turkish cuisine."

Our menu was exciting: Turkish Spicy Eggplant Salad, Poached Dried Apricots Filled with Yogurt Cream and Sprinkled with Pistachios, Swiss Chard Stuffed with Lamb and Herbs, Gülümay's Walnut-Garlic Spread with Hot and Sweet Peppers and Pomegranate Syrup, and Yufka—Peasant Flat Bread Baked on a Griddle.

Yufka, a type of bread that has been eaten by the Turkish people for centuries, was the first dish we cooked. Everyone had a hand in rolling the dough into thin round pieces ready for Gretchen's hot griddle, turning it as it started to bubble, and smelling it as the dough cooked through. With enough yufka stacked for our meal later, we all broke off pieces and enjoyed the fresh taste of this ancient bread.

I took a bite and closed my eyes. I was transported to a tribal village high in the Taurus Mountains of southern Turkey. Three years ago, in a stone hut with a griddle situated over a slow but steady fire, I knelt with a nomad woman making yufka. She pinched off a piece of dough from a tin bowl beneath the foot high table, and with a weathered rod rolled the dough into a thin oval. She picked it up and laid it on the griddle to cook.

When she finished, she gave me the rod. I pinched off a piece of dough, and rolled it carefully into a shapeless pathetic pancake. She scooted over, placed her brown hands over mine, and together we rolled out a perfect round of yufka. As it cooked on the griddle, she took one from the stack near her, tore it into pieces and handed one to me. We ate the bread, talked of cooking and drank our tea. We could have been two women in Gretchen Allison's kitchen on San Juan Island. We could have been in a hut in southern Turkey.

I propose a Turkish toast—to making bread together, to breaking bread together for a thousand more years—Şerefe.

A Baja Rain

The rain comes in sheets, sideways on the wind. It streams in rivulets from the red tile roof and snares itself in the masses of ruby bougainvillea that hug the wall. The sea and sky meld into a single grayness.

The surf on the Sea of Cortez pounds the shore in a tantrum but my eyes are on the sequined drops that dance from the Baja sky.

The mountains behind me, without a haze of dust between us, have marched closer. The rains have washed the dusty palm fronds clean. The cacti stands tall, the oleander bends low in the gusts.

I fling the patio door open and breathe in big gulps of moist air. The rain pelts my face and puddles at my feet. I tiptoe across the tiled floor to the front door, prop it firmly open. Today this place will smell like the wet of home.

I have just read in a local magazine that the average rainfall in this area is seven inches a year. Seven. It is possible I will have been here for this year's entire annual rainfall.

I wave a wet hand for attention. "John, I know what my problem is."

John searches for a cereal bowl. "Didn't know you had one." His T-shirt is an old sorority Dad's Day shirt from Anna's college days. His blue shorts are perfect for this weather.

"It's still February. I need to see you in a flannel shirt, a vest, maybe a little moss growing on your cap."

He adds milk to his oatmeal and gives it the taste test. "Ah, you want to go home."

"Yes." I tilt my nose into the air. "Just smell this rain. Four weeks of sand, sun, dry air. I've had enough."

His spoon stops its ascension. "You want to go now?"

"Yes. I need trees, swans, my slippers, and if I'm lucky, that old stray cat."

Later, when the rains have disappeared and cotton ball clouds dot the azure sky, John appears in front of me with a tall drink and a piece of paper.

"Day after tomorrow," he says. "There's an afternoon flight that arrives in Seattle too late for us to get to the ferry, but we'll be home on Friday. That work for you?"

"Yes."

He has done this for me, and I quietly thank him. We've had a good time here, but home is calling and I want to answer it on the first ring.

Solar Power

We heard it on our first morning home, sitting at the breakfast table. The cat door leading from the patio into the mud room fluttered open.

I leaned forward to get a view through the inner glass door. "Guess who is still here."

"No kidding," John was hoping so for my sake. "I'm glad."

In a flash I had swooped the cat up into a big hug. "Miss me?" I purred. He butted my head with his own. I grabbed my blanket and settled the both of us into the rocking chair, closed my eyes and stretched my feet out upon the hearth.

I ran my fingers down his legs, feeling the power under his thick fur. Deep in his throat, he rumbled like an old diesel train.

"You are a '68 GTO," I told him. "All muscle and 'tude." His tail flipped in a snappy rhythm.

"That cat is a heat seeking lump," John interjected realism into my morning. "It isn't you he wants. He's a solar powered cat that follows the sun. You're about to be as un-important as yesterday's news."

"Don't think so. Can't you hear us communing?" I'm in

cat-love.

"Right," John slits another envelope and continues reading the mountain of mail.

On some level I know that in the mouth of this cat's life I might be a temporary filling. I tell John I want to stick a cat cam on his head and see where he goes. John swears I really don't want to know.

"He's smart." John says, nodding in the cat's direction. "First it was the porch, then the mud room, now it's a bed and a lap in the kitchen. What next?"

What could I say? Maybe he has four homes and six girl-friends (platonic, I'm sure) scattered around the island. All I know is when he shows up and rubs my robe, threads himself between my ankles, climbs into my lap, stretches out with both paws on my shoulder, gives me that green eyed it-doesn't-matter-where-I've-been-I'm-with-you-now look and turns on his throaty purring machine, I melt.

In a few moments, whiskers twitching, he is asleep in my arms. I believe the stray cat has found his home.

"Tuxedo," I look at John. "What do you think about that for a name?"

"Sounds good."

Just that fast an internal alarm jolted the newly named Tuxedo awake. He sat up, yawned and slipped off my lap. Without a backward glance he sauntered to a nearby sun drenched chair, gently leapt into it, wound himself into a coil and covered his nose with his tail.

John, wise man that he is, said nothing.

Winter

Spring

Spring

A Tidbit Of Spring

I'm jazzed. Winter is over according to my calendar, and boy-oh-boy—spring is in the wings. The big blow this past weekend cleaned out the last of the fragile tree branches that were weakened in the winter storms, and deposited them helter-skelter on the patio. I notice that our old canoe, who has spent her winter face down on our dock, has been flipped over into the lake. It seems Mother Nature is doing a little spring cleaning.

Earlier, at the marina in town, most of the boats were still buttoned up in winter covers, waiting to unfurl and billow. A solitary figure, hunched down into his coat, trudged past me on the dock. A gust of wind caused my ears to tingle and I quickly headed up Spring Street to finish my errands.

At King's Marine, I heard a voice from deep within a stack of boxes proclaim that everything was 40% off. Winter is now at a deep discount. We're sending her on her way with a big sales event. I collected my few items, totted up the total and shivered my way toward the car. "Not so springy today," I spoke to a passenger in the next auto, who nodded his head in agreement.

Spring

At Market Place I found bright primroses begging for a window box or garden spot in which to pose. It stirred my blood. A trowel and some rich dirt could start me humming.

On my way home, the sun burst through the clouds and shone over the meadows and on the winery buildings at San Juan Vineyards. An SUV, headed toward town, had pulled over—two children were hanging out the window. Our island camel was munching, carefully ignoring the pack of humans. I checked my rearview mirror to see that no one was coming, pulled over to the road's edge and rolled down my window. "Her name is Mona."

The father relayed that to the children, and the mother asked how she got here. (Note to self: Mona needs her own interview.) I filled them in with what I know and noticed that with our two autos stopped, Mona was nonchalantly heading for the fence, as if there might be an apple in the gathering.

"Tell her she's beautiful." I suggested. "She loves to be admired." I pulled away and realized that Mona's fan club had started early in this new season.

At our house, the plum trees refuse to be called victims of the winter storm. They have defiantly embraced their odd new shapes. A close inspection reveals plump buds and a healthy attitude for growth, uh-huh.

There are two large loaves of banana bread in my oven at this moment. Granny Smith apples sit in the pantry awaiting a deep-dish pie pan and a crusty blanket of dough. A lamb roast thaws in the refrigerator and fresh eggs, soon to be deviled, bubble in a copper pot.

I have just enough time to slip down to the lake where two

swans feed near our dock. They glide among the ducks. Swans and ducks are in total agreement today over what portion of the lake belongs to whom.

"You never tell me when you're leaving," I say to the swans, "so if you're gone tomorrow, have a great spring and summer. We'll be here when you get back."

The sun warms me on the way up the hill. There is a lot more of it these days. Another of the reasons, I am sure, for the bounce in my step.

John pops in the house fresh from an errand. "What's that I smell?"

"It's banana bread aroma trying to escape," I explain as I slip out of my shoes. "Have you noticed how it hovers around the doorjamb and tickles your nose when you come in?"

He sets another carton of Heidi eggs on the table. "You're peppy today. What's up?"

"Spring's up, that's what. Not all the way, I know, but enough to make me feel the push of new birth."

"And all the food is for?"

"Days when plants and dirt regain their rightful place in the hierarchy of the seasons and I won't want to cook."

An appetizer of spring is what we're having. A tidbit to tide us over until the entrée arrives. I'm ready. Woot, woot!

Spring

Nature's March Madness

Mother Nature is snippy today. A few days of sun, a slap of rain mixed with high winds and then a vague threat of snow. Spring will arrive when I'm ready, she says in a blowsy tiff.

The new buds and blossoms of March ignore her huffy ways. They gang up on trees and shrubs in defiant colors. Impatient flowers pop their heads up from the wet earth and high-five each other in the gusting wind. We are here they shout in a collective voice, and more of us are coming every day!

March is the exuberant child. She bursts out before winter is completely over, shaking off the drab of February like a dog sheds water. I'm here now, she crows, without a single backward glance toward the dullness of winter.

"Forty-four new lambs," our friend Colleen sings into the phone, "you should come out." I slide on my waterproof boots, and John and I head for the farm. We troop to the barn as Colleen calls three hesitant lambs to her to share a large bottle of milk. They jostle for position, slurping hungrily as she evenly feeds them under the watchful eye of a tired but appreciative mother.

Spring

In the pasture more lambs are soaking up the sunny rays. Ewes are munching new shoots of grass, never far from their little ones. A tiny white lamb with a smooth black face plants her hooves firmly into the wet soil, stretches for a teat and closes her eyes in success.

We bounce homeward in our old truck and I glance at our lake as we drive by. The swans have taken their leave. I am always saddened by this final act of winter, but in their stead will be longer days, hummingbirds and other rites of spring.

I decide March might be my favorite month. With unapologetic fervor she pushes her way to the front of the spring parade. I want to lead she yells. A wearied Mother Nature smiles and nods.

The Art of Gardening

There is a lone azalea bush in my lower garden. Stubborn, scrubby, it clung to life for the three years we owned but didn't live in our home. I have tended it carefully in the years since. This spring it is awash in a mass of pink blossoms.

When I asked a gardening friend for some suggestions to landscape the ever growing beds, composted and ready for new life, she said, "You might consider moving that azalea."

"Can't do that, reminds me of my Mother. A Mississippi flower dressed in pink. Got to work around it." The sight of my mother in her little visor and sunglasses, bent over an aza-lea bush, is too strong a memory to relegate this bush to a place where I can't see it every morning.

We walked to the front of the house and she pointed to a tree in a north flower bed. "How about that tree?"

"Can't, John's favorite, has to stay."

She gave me the teacher-student look over her glasses. "This isn't going to be a 'plant-in-threes, coordinate-your-colors kind of garden' is it?"

I kicked a stone, stuffed my hands deep into my pockets. "I thought I wanted a garden like the ones in *Fine Gardening* magazine." I kicked another stone harder. "But I don't."

What I *do* want came to me on Monday as John and I sat in the overflowing memorial service for Steve Swanberg. The Presbyterian church was filled with big shouldered men in riotously colored Hawaiian shirts.

After the service, a multitude of friends gathered at the Yacht Club for a continued celebration of Steve's life. I watched those shirts buzzing among each other. One group of four shirts—red, orange, green and blue—stirred the pot of remembrance and between bursts of wistful laughter retold a familiar story that bubbled its way to the top.

I decided that day I wanted my garden to be like Steve's vast array of friends. I want short and tall combos, early and late-bloomers, vibrant splashes of in-your-face annuals buoyed up by the muted shades of time-tested perennials.

Steve, thanks to you the stubborn azalea stays—not part of a trio, just a single feisty shrub. I just might plant a screaming yellow something-or-other next to it. The chance for color-coordinated flowers underneath John's tree? Not going to happen.

Later this spring, when I've finished introducing the plants into my garden that make me happy, have plowed my hands deep into rich smelling earth and touched tender leaves that unfold gently in the morning sun, then I will see a palette of colors and a pattern that is a true reflection of who I am.

Steven Fulton Swanberg—a master of well tended friend-ships—has taught me the art of gardening.

Deer Gazing

"I'm taking the tractor down to get a load of logs for the log splitter," John says as he opens the door. He freezes in mid-step. "Maybe not," he motions to me. A doe, curled tight in a circle of sunlight, sleeps on the long arm of a rock that slopes toward our bedroom window. She is framed by stately evergreens and the blotchy splayed arms of a bronze madrona. We watch her flick her ears and adjust her head to a more comfortable position.

"It can wait." John tosses his cap on the table. We walk quietly to our bedroom window for a closer view. A flowering plum tree just outside offers us pink camouflage. Two years ago a doe used this same spot to recover, I think, from the exhaustion of birth.

"Yesterday I started out the back gate to check the box-woods and startled a doe," I whispered. "She was bigger, all curled up in that little place by the path to the lake." The back of our house remains thick with salal and trees. A heavily matted patch of grass speaks to the comfortableness found by the deer that meander through our acreage.

We have stood in quiet awe before: a certain black fox

waves his white tipped tail as he trots past our front door; a large woodpecker and two juveniles attack a dead stump in our yard, the rat-a-tat-tatting reverberates throughout the house; and a resident bald eagle fishes in the lake from the tallest perch on Roy Island.

The doe rouses and begins to graze her way down the rock. "Could be a while before she's through," John reasons. "Give her plenty of time to finish." We back away from the window and retreat to the living room where a boating magazine captures John's attention. I dash off a quick note to a friend.

Placing stamps on the last of the notes, I look out the window to find the doe has wandered on. I pick up John's cap and hand it to him. "I think I hear the logs calling." We both stand for a moment in the open door, look toward the rock where the doe has slept and smile at each other.

In exchange for a few moments of accommodating her needs, a doe gives us a sun dappled moment to remember.

On Tour

John and I have returned from a trip to be greeted by a garden gone wild in our absence and a temperature colder than St. Petersburg, Russia. Not quite ready to tackle the garden, nor the laundry, I am delighted to check the calendar and find the San Juan Island Artists' Studio Tour slated for the weekend.

John checks out the map on the brochure. "Let's start south and work our way back into town." We wait for a doe to meander out of the driveway. "So, what's our first stop?"

"Mary Gey McCulloch," I say. I read parts of the brochure aloud. "She's got Rudi and Bill Weissinger there, and two more artists I don't know." I look at him out of the corner of my eye. "One stop shopping." I wait for his slight cough that generally follows the word shopping—ah—there it is.

We arrive and find Fred McCulloch out front artistically directing car traffic. Just inside the gate, I stop to take in the sight of Mary's garden. Many of the flowers are eye-level and blooming in profusion. I follow the paths, and see the reds, oranges and blues of her garden reflected in the boldness and spontaneity of her paintings, all situated in the garden itself. Her work seems to say, life is for the here and now!

Arranged in the center of the garden are various pieces sculpted by Bill Weissinger.

"Okay to touch?" I ask. I want to lay my cheek against the side of two sleek salmon and feel the coldness of the stone. Each of the pieces, some whimsical, some poetic, evoke a different response. One in particular, featuring three stone thrones, makes me pause. It reminds me of the small lighted children's chairs at the Oklahoma City Bombing Memorial.

Out of the garden and along the studio wall, Rudi Weissinger's paintings are displayed. Her years at a loom are captured within the complex layering of color and intensity that begs a closer inspection.

Inside the studio, Margaret Thorson showcases the love of weaving in her pastel, soft-as-goose-down hats, and in the rugs she chooses to exhibit. At the other end, Nancy Lind captures light and color in an extensive array of show-stopping jewelry.

"There is no end to the talent on these islands," I say to John on our way to the car. "Where do they find their unique inspiration?"

We wander back to town and stop at Ann Walbert's studio. There, a pastoral view of green meadows and a deep sense of calm prevails, in spite of the gusty wind. Inside, hot coffee, fruit and cookies await us. I had bypassed the treats earlier, but the steaming cup of coffee Ann offers only adds to the enjoyment of her art.

"I love these sheep," I tell Ann, of a particular piece.

A long conversation later, I wander to the house, where John has joined Ann's husband, along with Mary Sly and Dan Wyatt of San Juan Silk. I lose myself in the rack of coats and vests. The deep purples, blues and reds of the coats and vests call to me. Mary helps me slip into one of them. Oh, my. Oh, yes.

"I custom make these too," she says as I survey the length.

I reluctantly take myself out of the shimmering coat. I could perhaps make my case for an anniversary or Christmas present, but I had told myself that earlier at Mary McCollough's too.

Across the room, Riki Schumacher is showing her jewelry to a visitor. Her remarkable metalwork alone makes each necklace a conversation piece.

This year is no exception. We have seen the incredible breadth and depth of the artistry of eight of our island friends and residents.

Back at the house, it is time to go to work. I stoop to pick up a pile of dirty clothes. A hummingbird flits by the window on his way to the feeder. I stop to watch eight brown ducklings swim by on the wind-rippled lake and realize I have the answer to my own question about the artists.

They find their inspiration to create from the lives they lead and the joy they find in simply living in these islands. It is enough.

Spring

Island Mothers

I glanced at the calendar last evening and turned to the fast approaching month of May. It's time to give myself a head's up for the birthdays and anniversaries I need to acknowledge.

I looked at the notation for Mother's Day. I'm happy to live in a place where we don't need such a reminder. Motherhood, in all its glory, is popping out all over.

A walk around my garden is enough to cause me to pause and reflect on the newness of life. The ground cover I hoped would spread between the walking stones has done so. The azalea bush is laden with tiny buds, the hydrangeas have the freshness of new leaves, and the hostas are sturdy green shoots rising up to join the spring procession.

Almost daily now, I see our yard deer graze across the lawn. Two are heavy with the weight of soon-to-be new life. I look forward, as in years past, to when the exhausted mothers will rest, after giving birth, in the soft mossy hollow of the large rock that stands sentinel over our driveway.

A trip around the island gives cause to stop and admire gangly new lambs. On Roche Harbor Road, two of them smack and suckle in newly found lamb nirvana. Soon, when I wander down to the lake, I'll be scolded by protective mother ducks as tiny trains of ducklings paddle fiercely away from our dock. Later, the empty robin's nest just outside our guest-house window will welcome sky blue eggs. The red-breasted mother will warm them until they poke and crackle their way to life.

Earlier this week, we shared the delight of a favorite young couple welcoming a healthy young son with perfectly formed toes and a flower-petal mouth into the world.

Islanders don't need a calendar to know that we are surrounded by females of all kinds who are feathering their nests, feeding their young and basking in the glow of motherhood.

Guest House

I snap the sheets, tuck them firmly under the mattress and swipe my hand across the taut surface. A quarter would indeed bounce. A quick toss of a summer-weight comforter and that's that.

The windows are open in the guesthouse. The golden chain tree is humming with bees, and I stand close to the window to suck in the fresh sweet smell that hovers in an invisible cloud. A doe, followed closely by a tottering new fawn, tiptoes over the driveway to the portion of my garden I share with her and her friends. I look down from my second story perch as she glances around before she bends her head for a slow nibble.

"Make a deal with you," I tell her. "I've got guests coming. Eat all you want but show up tomorrow about seven. Give 'em a thrill."

She flicks her ears and tail. I'm not sure if that's a yes or no. Historically I can't depend on our yard deer to do as I ask. More often, they have surprised me and my guests with memorable moments of their own volition.

I look around. I feel like I'm in a tree house with window boxes. There is a sweeping view of the lawn, circular driveway, woods and deep salal beyond. A step into the living room highlights the lake traffic. Geese, ducks, and an occasional kayak float by on their journey around Roy Island.

The sofa looks inviting. I sit down and pick up the leather-bound guestbook from the coffee table. I blow a tornado of dust off its cover—which will be shining before I leave—and flip through the pages.

Each entry is complete with a photograph of our guests and their favorite island places. Some leave behind images of the pick-up-sticks pile of driftwood on South Beach; others prefer Lime Kiln Park and a chance viewing of the whales; still others the ferry and a floatplane in busy Friday Harbor. Some wanted a photo of themselves in our canoe on the lake or sitting in the giant branches of the elderly fir just off our patio.

The pages of the guestbook remind me we have hosted two sets of honeymooners, two couples celebrating wedding anniversaries and countless friends and family from around the country and the world.

"Never had a deer come up on the patio while I was drinking coffee before," says a big city friend.

"From one islander to another, keep it rural," writes another who hails from Guernsey.

"Love the cool weather," pens my cousin from New Delhi. "Book me for next year."

Each page and notation brings back a river of memories. One friend has passed away since he visited. How glad John and I are to have a picture of him at the Front Street Café, coffee in hand as we waited with him for the ferry.

Spring

I close the book and look from the living room window toward the lake. Each of our visitors have left this island and recorded a memory for me that I can share with those who have yet to come.

"Tomorrow evening, seven sharp," I remind the doe. I sweep and dust the guesthouse with renewed vigor.

Another summer has arrived, and with it an opportunity to view our island life through the eyes of others.

Summer

Summer

Glory Days

In a full-tilt spin toward summer, long days have grown into dazzling stalks of sunlight. Outside projects, like warm yeasty dough, have doubled in size throughout the spring.

School has gasped its last breath, and kids have flung their books and backpacks into the nearest corner to fight it out with dust bunnies for another summer. Friends, vacation, camp and sleep are the order of the day.

Trips to town along Roche Harbor Road require a watchful eye. Gaggles of bicyclists and kayak-crowned cars stop to photograph Mona Camel, her head over the fence in a feed-me-for-a-picture pose. Fame has its advantages.

The engines of commerce are humming. Desultory chatter about spring rains has been replaced with crisp efficiency at the cash registers as visitors stream through local stores and restaurants. Friday Harbor hats and shirts adorn folks who stop mid-crossing on Spring Street to consult a map, their camera in hand.

At our house, the lake sparkles and our old canoe lazes on the dock. At water's edge, a mother duck thinks I am too near. She scolds me as she splashes her way toward the middle of the lake while six frenzied ducklings echo her displeasure.

On the patio, the chaise lounge sulks in the corner waiting for her turn in the sun. I'll get to you, I say as I sweep around her legs and fold the coverings that have kept her clean over the winter. Be patient.

Later, a breeze from the open window teases the white curtain—and me. Tuxedo is asleep in his captain's chair. I glance up from the computer and long to be out on this perfect day. Why not? I can pull a weed or two and clear my mind. I call the cat and he comes, jumps up on the patio ledge to guard me. Down in the lower garden, I yank small stubborn weeds from among the hostas, wild ginger and rose bushes. When I stop to sit, Tux deigns to join me. He stretches the length of my lap and lowers his head for a welcome snooze. Looks like a good thing to do. I lean back against the garden wall and turn my face to the sun.

Laughter drifts from the far side of the lake and a plane drones overhead. A thought keeps nagging at me. I scoop the cat up and off my lap and make my way back to the sulking chaise lounge. It's time. I shake her pillows and arrange her just so, plop down and stretch out. Tuxedo joins me.

Now, that's better. Everyone and everything deserves to share in these glory days.

Ask Me, I Live Here

The San Juan Islands Ambassadors have been selected. I am delighted to be the program coordinator working with these young teens in training in the hospitality industry to assist our visitors with answers to questions on restaurants and lodging, destinations sites, map reading, transportation and general questions. Their stations of duty will include Friday Harbor, Roche Harbor and selected ferry runs from Anacortes.

This past Sunday we gathered at San Juan Excursions for our first training event, a whale watching trip.

"Your job," I told them before boarding, "is two-fold. First, enjoy the trip from the perspective of a tourist, and second, observe the tourists on board. Write down your observations and give them to me at the end of the trip."

For four hours I observed the observers observing the observees. I wondered which group of people, tourists or Ambassadors, would ultimately be most affected by this expedition.

The following are excerpts I collected at the end of the excursion:

"The tourists seemed very interested and willing to learn.

When we saw the whales they got very excited, and their excitement got me excited."

"Being among tourists was nothing new for me, but observing them was new. I noticed many unique qualities that are often skipped by locals. These tourists were fairly quiet and observed everything with genuine interest. Every time the guides on the boat had something to say the tourists hung on every word, trying hard to understand our foreign island area."

"When they saw whales they got so excited they flocked to the front of the boat. They kept their eyes wide open, looking all around. Overall, though, the tourists are difficult to predict."

"The tourists were somehow surprisingly concerned with the history of the region. A totally unexpected question as to the population of the islands was posed only a few minutes into the trip."

"Tourists differ from one another in that some of them are interested in 'wild' life and some are interested in 'night' life."

"Tourists seem to be very understanding and carefree in nature. In appearance, they tend to be prepared for any occurrence. In fact, they are all dressed warmly and have expressed foresight, by that they have every amenity conceivable for this expedition."

"Every time the whales came up the tourists would either scream or jump. This must be because they live in Texas."

Stay tuned. It's going to be a great summer!

Catching the Rays

There is not a cloud to be seen in the sky, maybe not in the western hemisphere. I know because I have searched long and hard before sitting down to write this column. What joy!

I have to share this with someone, and John isn't here at the moment. "Hey Tuxedo." I leave the computer and walk to the living room door. Tuxedo is in his lounge chair, flat on his back with all four white tipped paws in the air. His tail is flipped over the arm of the chair. A wide shaft of sunlight is cooking him to warm perfection.

I stroll over and bend down to within inches of his whiskered face. "I'm talking to you, kiddo."

"Whaaaat?" He yawns and the aroma of morning-old tuna smacks me in the face. One green eye opens.

"It's gorgeous outside. I'm going out, come on." I set my straw hat firmly on my head. "You can fish in the lake, hunt for mice in the woods, walk with me to the mailbox." I rub his belly. "Get outside and do something."

"You're kidding." Now both eyes hold me in kindly contempt. "Waste this sun that's dancing on my belly?" He yawns again. "Where's the alpha male in the family? He'd understand."

"If John were here you'd both be asleep, but he's out in the fresh air and you should be too."

Tuxedo rolls over on his side and sighs deeply. He stretches once and closes me out of his life until I come to my senses.

"Ah, who needs you anyway?" I pull on my yard shoes and let the screen door bang on my way out.

Outside the air is crisp and mild. The lake, through the trees, sparkles like a sheet of party paper. I hear birds chittering away in idle gossip. Overhead the drone of an airplane causes me to look up and see a glint of silver as it wings its way southward.

I'm glad I'm not on that plane. This is where I want to be. Island living is the best. I walk down our winding lane and hear a woodpecker busy at work on a dead tree in the woods. I startle a doe crossing the drive and she high jumps her way out of sight. With a bundle of mail in hand, I re-trace my steps to the house.

"I'm back, and you missed a grand walk, you lazy cat." I drop the mail on the table and lean against the door. "You'll be sorry you missed this when the rains come again."

Tuxedo flicks his tail, the only sign he has heard a word I've said. Once again he is on his back, his belly an invitation to the sun. He yawns again. "Who needs to be out in it to enjoy it? To each his own."

A Conversation with Mona

There are certain signals of summer's arrival on the island that have nothing to do with kayaks, lambs, or the baskets of flowers that hang in splendor from the light poles in town. One that I watch with great interest is the number of cars that stop along Roche Harbor Road to get a good look and a photo of our island celebrity, Miss Mona Camel.

I was fortunate to be granted an interview, and the following is a transcript of our conversation.

MK: Good morning, Mona. Thank you for spending a few minutes with me.

Mona: Good morning to you. First, it's imperative that you know I'm a dromedary camel and not a Bactrian camel. So, let's just get that little bit of information out of the way up front, shall we?

MK: We shall. I know you're a dromedary camel because you have one hump and Bactrians have two humps. Most people around the world just call you a camel. Does that bother you?

Mona: Not in the least. I just wanted it down for the record. You are writing this down, aren't you?

MK: But of course. I've noticed an increase in visitors stopping by to see you. It won't be long before you'll be back in the height of summer lime-light. Are you looking forward to another summer of celebrity?

Mona: Yes. I actually enjoy the tourists—most days, anyway. Some days I ignore them—I'm allowed, you know. Celebrity and all that. On the other hoof, some offer food . . .

MK: They should know you have other things to do, but I have noticed some people do stop and offer you food. What do you prefer?

Mona: Well, I think you know my friend Jack McKenna. He's that cutie that stops here every day with the best food, let me tell you—where were we—I adore pears. I like apples, oranges and bananas—but only if you peel them. Oh yes, I'll bury my face up to my eyelashes in a big slice of watermelon. Umm, I can't wait. This doesn't make me a fruititarian, you understand, because I eat celery and lettuce occasionally. Oh yes, I love small yellow potatoes too.

MK: What are your least favorite foods?

Mona: I abhor eggplant. Cannot stand any kind of peppers, asparagus—is that a food?—and onions—bad breath you know.

MK: Does your diet include fruit with pits?

Mona: Oh yes, I eat the fruit and spit out the pits. I have sharp front teeth, powerful grinders in the back, and none in between. Keeps the dental bills down considerably.

MK: So you're a pit spitter.

Mona: Yes, indeedy.

MK: Change of topic. Do you enjoy having your photo taken?

Mona: I do. I actually have a "better side." Let me turn and I'll show you. See?

MK: Now that you mention it, I do. I've always heard camels have the longest eyelashes. May I look at yours?

Mona: Knock yourself out. Wait, I'll bat them for you.

MK: Well, it is absolutely true, and I'm envious. Your lashes are incredible. Let me step back a bit. Has anyone ever mentioned camel breath to you?

Mona: It's the price you pay to stare at my lashes. The key is to stay upwind. Works like a charm.

MK: Mona, are you happy here on San Juan Island?

Mona: Heavens yes. There's the vineyard over there and occasionally I get a whiff when there's a group enjoying themselves; it's quite heady, actually. That owner has me on a label, Mona Vino, can you imagine? And then, I have this wonderful

pasture, what's not to love? People stop to visit
and Jack McKenna sweet talks me every single
day.

MK: Well, it's been great talking with you, Mona. I
hope you have a wonderful summer.

Mona: You're so welcome. Do you have an apple on
you? Or better yet, a pear? Never mind, I see
Jack coming.

Not to be Forgotten

On July 4th, 2000, we gathered up our children, grandchildren and Astrid, our exchange student from Germany, along with folding chairs and bottles of water and set up on the corner of Blair and Spring Street to watch the parade.

This is *the* summer event of the year, and throngs of islanders and visitors alike streamed along Spring Street searching amid red white and blue banners and bunting for a place to watch our parade extravaganza. There were 58 entries in the parade that year. I know because Astrid took a picture of each and every one of them.

"Look at that," she hooted, pointing to the brand-spanking new lawnmower/tractor making circle eights in the street. "We would *never* do that in Werlte, or anywhere else in Germany." She aimed her camera square at the mower. "I love this parade!"

I remember that moment. I'm sure it was Darren from the Harbor Saw Shop scooting around the street, giving the mower a little gas to let it roar. That was it for Astrid. Nothing else came close to her mower-in-the-parade experience.

There were many other entries to enjoy. Each family member came away with a float that wowed them. We climbed over each other's conversation in our quest to get our personal favorite selected as "Best of" in the "Not-To-Be-Forgotten-Fourth-of-July-Happy-Birthday-America-Parade."

Later, we strolled to the Picnic at the Historical Museum, ate the best of wursts and sat on the lawn with sodas teetering on the grass about us.

Back home, we seized spoons and quickly mobilized the ever ready Pots-and-Pans Band. Astrid was the Grand Marshal for our raucous parade around the circular drive.

In a late evening orange afterglow we headed out to Roche Harbor and trouped down the dock to our old boat.

Clambering aboard, we smelled the sizzle and watched the spew of fireworks that thundered upward into a blue-black sky. Appropriate ooohhs and aaahhhhs accompanied each gigantic burst.

Driving home, spent and exhausted from a long day of celebration I asked Astrid, "So, what part of the day did you like best?"

She bobbed her head and her white blond hair swayed sideways. "The parade, the real parade, you know, in town—it was the best."

A few days ago John received a birthday greeting from Astrid. She is currently working on her thesis for her university diploma in Cologne, Germany. She wrote us of her life and travels and then added a wistful note:

"I wish I could be at the parade next week! That was so much fun!"

Seven years ago, Darren on a lawnmower and 57 other entries showcased how we celebrate our nation's birth in a "Not-to-Be-Forgotten-Fourth-of-July-Happy-Birthday-America Parade."

I echo Astrid's sentiment. Our parade, you know, in town, it *is* the best.

Summer

The Good Health Team

This isn't the summer I planned back in the winter when visions of my garden in bloom kept many a dreary morning at bay. I thought I would be elbow deep in grandchildren, boating and summer salads, enjoying those perfect days to match our perfect summer weather.

Instead, an annual health test revealed an abnormality, followed by a biopsy, appointments with specialists, surgery and now, horizontal time I didn't expect.

John and I arrived home this past Sunday to find that in our week long absence friends had decidedly taken matters of our good health into their own hands. By the time he had me ensconced in the bedroom, the first in a series of friends appeared with a hot delicious meal. This phenomenon would continue for several days.

We didn't know who would appear at our door each evening armed with glazed casserole dishes, still steaming from the kitchen; baskets of just-picked strawberries and raspberries; loaves of warm bread; cold bowls of healthy green salads; and slices of scrumptious desserts. It takes great effort, time and care to put together and deliver such meals.

Other friends bolstered my mental health with thoughtful selections of books and magazines. They understand the boredom of bed rest. There were those who came to sit in companionable silence, fully aware that conversation is not the ruler by which friendship is measured.

The slightest breeze still wafts the scent from the hand-picked bouquets of peonies, Sweet Williams and fragrant honeysuckle situated throughout the house. The professional arrangement from our local florist sits in a fashionable droop, its lighter scent a separate pleasure to enjoy. What spirit doesn't rise at nature's perfume?

The Good Health Team didn't stop there. They mailed cards and notes, telephoned, winged e-mails harboring little bursts of encouragement, and in general reminded me that I am not forgotten. With such care and concern, the road to wellness is more easily traveled.

A friend of ours is off-island as we speak, preparing for surgery and a long recovery at home. I can't cook yet, so John has volunteered to make a meal, buy a card, sit a spell or run an errand. It's our turn to be a part of the good health cycle of our island.

The Upside of Down Time

A doe caught in a brown-eyed moment stands framed between the proud-standing daisies and a ring of silver Dusty Miller in my front garden. She has been nosing around with her still-spotted fawn every day now for weeks. They hunt for succulent weeds, blossoms and tender shoots of their favorite shrubs.

I roll open the window and talk to her. "What's up, Mom?"

She doesn't leave, but rises on her hind legs for a bite of River Birch leaves.

"I'll get John to cut some of those scraggly ones down for you." In my physician-imposed-house-bound state I've developed a special kinship with these two that feed outside my window.

The bees in front of my north window are humming about a catmint convention, and the doe has grazed over to the front of our shed and stretches out in a shaft of sunlight. She closes her eyes and lowers her head to rest on the grass. A flick of an ear is her only movement. Baby nibbles nearby. In a few minutes, they change places, and the fawn lies down in the mother-warmed grass.

On another day, I move to the south facing patio and sit back in the chaise lounge and well, lounge. I have my book, *Birding in the San Juan Islands* by Mark G. Lewis and Fred A. Sharpe, binoculars and wide brimmed hat. Blue dragon flies hover overhead like delicate helicopters. In a short time, I spot a Red-breasted Nuthatch and later, a Red Crossbill perched on a limb of a hefty pine tree. There are chirps and warbles, caws and nyak, nyak, nyaking from every direction. I bird watch until my neck needs a rest and a nap is imminent.

Later, at my nudging, John checks out the lower level of our inner garden. He returns with four purple-red roses, fresh from our old-fashioned climbing rose vine. I place them in a cobalt blue vase and stick a banana-yellow rose bud in the center. This is my version of summer color.

I would have missed these scenes had I had the busy summer I planned for myself—one filled with guests, children, crabbing, boating and tightening the threads of family and friends. Instead, I have enjoyed the nature that abounds on this lake and acreage on which I live.

A few mandated weeks in the not-so-fast lane have left me refreshed and renewed. There is a wheelbarrow full of summer remaining, and I'm ready.

Vacation

Our daughter Chrissy has arrived for a whirlwind visit. For her abbreviated stay we have put together a fast-moving scenario of options and offered it to her for her perusal.

She glances at it. "Take me everywhere and show me everything."

"Can't do that, but this weekend has some of everything." We slide into the old banged up Geo we call "the Grape" and carefully avoid the bicycles and too-fast cars zooming along Roche Harbor Road.

On the hill above Roche Harbor, I pull off the road and show Chrissy what may be the most photographed view of the harbor. The morning sun has splashed brightness on the boats and it ricochets across the sky and water. Down in the village, San Juan Island Ambassadors Ashleigh and Catlyn, smartly dressed and smiling, answer Chrissy's myriad questions.

We dink around the hotel, grounds, and kiosks full of art, jewelry, photography and knitwear. We walk along the docks to see the dazzling array of mega-yacht-to-what-you-got size boats. Sated with a chocolate ice cream cone, we move on to the canopy of green that greets us as we drive along West Valley Road. We scoot out to the pastoral tranquility of Krystal Acres and commune with the alpacas grazing along the fence row.

At Lime Kiln Park, we claim an empty picnic table to enjoy the view and wave to exuberant kayakers intent on their destination. Their peals of laughter skim across the water.

"Think they're having fun?" Chrissy laughs in return. "Speaking of fun, how about a picture of me and the lighthouse?"

"Stand right there if you want it perfectly centered at the top of your head," I say. Collectively we have pictures of spires and edifices from around the world protruding from between our ears, and this one needs to be added to the collection.

On our way again we stop to let a tiny fawn commandeer the roadway for a moment. A small sigh from Chrissy reminds me this is indeed a special sight.

Down at South Beach, the rhythm of the waves, the dark sand and black-and-white Dalmatian stones weave their magic. Chrissy collects some large ones, weighs them in her hand, and reluctantly drops them back again. "Carry-on luggage," she says.

In town, sea planes roar a warning as they take off over Brown Island and ferries disgorge day-trippers, who mill about like bees, collecting souvenir pollen to take home to their respective hives.

We complete the circle tour, find our way home and sprawl on the sofas. "Tomorrow is going to be just as great," I tell her. "Look at all the things Dad has planned." I wiggle my toes and realize I too am anticipating the community theatre, whale watching, Lavender Festival, Summer Art Fair, art galleries and several favorite restaurants. I've gone on vacation without leaving home.

Summer

Crabbing

"Want to go with me to pick up the pot?" John had been over at the boat and dropped a crab pot to soak earlier in the day.

"Uh-huh." We crunch our way across the gravel drive.

Our parking area for the old truck is on an incline. Not up—sideways. For me, that means I clamber in on the uphill side. Then I stick my right foot out to stop the heavy door as it falls into a closed position. If I'm not careful, I will topple into the middle of the seat and smack the gear shift.

Securely in my seat without incident, we chug along Roche Harbor Road, counting eleven bicyclists. There will be another one around the curve—the rule of two—there she is, pedaling hard to catch up to the others. As we swing around onto West Valley Road, we slow down to watch an alpaca pose for a grateful tourist.

We feel the temperature drop in a low spot on Mitchell Bay Road and wind our way down to the marina at Snug Harbor. There is a cool breeze floating through the window and the air smells—how to describe it—the air smells good.

Down at the boat, we ease into the dinghy and swing out to our solitary pot.

John pulls in the line and lifts the wire square out of the water. "Let's see what we've got."

There is a tangle of claws. The turkey leg has done the trick. John dons his gloves and goes to work. "Too small, too small, too small," he drops three in quick succession over the side. "Female and another female." They too get dropped into the drink.

I look at the last two. Could be dinner.

John grapples with them. "A couple of big keepers." One clings to the wire bottom with one claw and makes a swipe at me with the other. I haven't brought my gloves and somehow this tough guy knows it. John maneuvers him out of the pot and drops him into the bucket.

We motor back to the boat, lift the dinghy up to its perch, grab the bucket and head for the truck.

"Let's drop one off for Jack and Heidi," John says as we rumble past our lane. "We only need one."

A crab to eat and one to share on a perfect summer day.

End of the Road

My summer with the San Juan Island Ambassadors has come to an end. And if I may say so, it was a hoot!

With thousands of inquiries among them, and hundreds of in-depth surveys collected to be used by the Chamber of Commerce, Visitors Bureau and other interested parties, they have proven their value in service to the community.

Work related stories within the ranks abound. I am told that one of the Island Ambassadors from last year was asked by a visiting Chicagoan about crime on the island. The Ambassador replied thoughtfully that while we didn't have drive-by shootings on the island, we did occasionally have drive-by arguments.

The following excerpts are from this year's end-of-season reports prepared by each ambassador in answer to various questions. I present them for your enjoyment.

"Be understanding of the visitors that come to the island and be patient with them. They are on vacation, and many times they have left their brains at home, so don't be rude to them if they are rude to you. Stay calm and you will find a solution."

The most rewarding part of this job is:

"The courage to talk to new people. Before this I would never talk to visitors and because I was forced to I am very comfortable with helping them."

"I helped a couple of travelers from South Africa. I was amazed because I used to live there and they lived in the same city I did. People from all over the globe come to visit the island."

"Gaining the experience that will help me later in life. I know more about my home than I did before. I was pushed to do my best, and I daresay I achieved it."

"I don't think I would ever have become so self-confident, or as easy with my peers, if not for this job."

"The reason this job should be done next year is the look on the visitors' faces. When you actually help them and they realize it, they recognize and appreciate you, even though they may have previously thought you were too young to know."

"The most memorable thing this summer was the uniform. I am confident that it will haunt me forever."

"If I could do it again, I would change the way that I went up to tourists. I would try to go up to them more instead of expecting them to come to me."

"My favorite part of the job was being out in the community and hearing how much shopkeepers and locals appreciated our services."

"My most interesting question was if the island had a brothel. It took me a while to recover from a question such as this one, and so I replied that I doubted it, but the Chamber of Commerce would know."

County Fair

The end of summer comes, not with the flip of a calendar month, but the bustle and humming of the San Juan County Fair.

For months, cooks have tweaked their apple pie recipes, held their jams and jellies up into the air looking for the perfect color. No old country brewer has spent more time tasting and testing his offering than the group of hopefuls who enter the county fair.

On the fairgrounds, a jaded old salt slowly wanders the fairgrounds and stands before a picture by a junior photographer. "Just look at that," he says. What he means is that the child has talent.

Our county fair belongs to everyone. In turn, our local attorneys, firefighters, accountants, city workers, county workers, retirees and young people submit their specialties. The attorney is a sculptor, the fireman a photographer, the county worker an artist, the student a baker and the tiny girl with a mass of blond curls a breeder of prize-winning chickens.

Every day of the fair folks attend to listen to our local musicians perform and stuff themselves with food made by the hands of friends.

The horseshoe shaped array of food booths are a must for the grazers. Take your pick: Elephant Ears, Berries'n Cream, gyros, burritos, egg rolls, snow cones, barbeque and the list goes on. Eat your fill and watch the kids scream in delight on the Tilt-A-Whirl, the Zipper and Para Trooper rides.

One year, after encouragement from my friend Amy, I entered the written word portion of the fair with a story and two poems. Everyone I had talked with was entering something, or had done so before, and the pride in garnering a ribbon was palpable.

I was in Juneau, Alaska when my friend Pam called me with the news. "You've won," she said. "I need to go and collect your entry and ribbons."

"Ribbons?" I was certain I had misunderstood.

"Yes, you've placed first in the short story contest and have a second and a third place in poetry."

Years later it's still a kick to know I have joined the ranks of the multitude of islanders who proudly say their summers have ended with a ribbon from the San Juan County Fair.

Summer

Autumn

Autumn

Autumn Teaser

It has been two weeks since the rains came and Mother Nature wrapped a foggy arm around Roy Island in a first-of-the-season embrace. This morning I moved my summer things—slid them down the closet rod to yesterday. I reached for a long sleeved shirt, rubbed the cotton flannel, slipped it on and chased the early morning chill away.

Tuxedo lays curled on a fleece throw in the corner of the sofa. He sniffs me cautiously. This is new, he grumbles. Sit still while I check you out.

"It's okay, Tux. Times, they are a changin', and your winter coat . . .," I pause to rub his black head and white belly, "is on its way." I scuff to the kitchen in my ratty red slippers and pour a cup of aromatic coffee.

Outside, a sheen of damp—like oil on a griddle—covers the back patio. Cup in hand, I step out into the smell of early morning. In the lower garden, I inspect the pear tree and drink in the scent of wet rich earth. I hear the splunk of raindrops on the hostas, a most welcome sound, and see tiny diamonds glinting in the thick fronds of fern. The lips of earth that frame our driveway are no longer parched but moist and full.

I wander down the path to the lake, step onto the creaky dock and sit down on the old orange canoe. Elvis, the neighboring rooster crows encouragement to a flock of geese as they wing their way toward a distant destination.

I have enjoyed the summer months of brilliant sunshine. But when the leaves begin their autumnal rustle and the morning air brings a certain chill, I am ready for the shirt, the vest and the heavier weight socks that signify a change in the rhythms of life.

Not just yet. The sun appears and warms the dock with a summer's morning heat. It is as if Mother Nature isn't ready to commit herself completely to this new season. In good time, she seems to say.

One evening in the days to come, when the porch lights cast a soft glow through the ivy leaves that drape them in fiery hues of red and brilliant gold, Autumn will return—perhaps as a gust of wind that scatters dried and crackling leaves at my door, or a damp gray blanket tucked low around the window sills. It may arrive as a high pitched whine down the chimney. But I will know—and in that moment, I will deeply bow and say, "Welcome autumn rain and fog. I've been expecting you."

Boating

It's a chance to celebrate. The throngs of summer boaters have left for who-knows-where and we, like many islanders, are out in force to re-claim our waters and all of British Columbia for ourselves.

In the years we have lived here, we have discovered the joy of time spent on our boat. From Juneau, Alaska to neighboring Garrison Bay we have dropped anchor in many harbors and coves. At times, we look for spots of seclusion, wanting nothing more than a good book, favorite beverage and companionable silence. At other times we enjoy the bustle of marinas, company of friends and time in favorite bookstores.

"Want to run up to Ganges?" John is ready to go.

"Oh, yeah." I toss my things into a canvas bag.

We motor out of Snug Harbor in the quiet of early morning. Haro Strait hosts a party of seals playing dunk-and-bob. The water is a blue-gray mirror, sparkling in the first rays of sun. A container ship passes, loaded with red, yellow, blue and green boxes headed north toward Vancouver. Global commerce is on the move.

John adjusts the GPS and sets our course for Ganges. He

leans against the bench seat in the pilot house and grins at me. "Nice out here, isn't it?"

"Very." My cup of coffee tastes good. I listen to the swoosh of water slicing by the bow. To our port side two graceful porpoise head south, intent on their destination. On other days they have pirouetted in front of our bow.

John points out the logs bumping along our way. "Need to watch for those deadheads." The wake of a solitary blue-hulled sailboat motoring along, its sails tightly furled, gives us a two-wave bounce. Sea gulls perch on a kelp bed, flapping their wings until they are in an all-heads-to-the-left chorus line pose.

We arrive at the point where the currents from San Juan Channel converge with the currents of Haro Strait. There is a swath of blue black water slap-dashing its way west, and we pick up a knot of speed as we pass through.

Up ahead, the Turn Point Light House rests, bathed in streaks of eastern sunlight. It is markedly different from the normal afternoon view with which I am familiar. On those days it is a stout, chest-thumping white sentry.

A low roar causes me to look toward a yellow float plane lifting out of the Strait. There is a flash of glint and sparkle off the left wing as it banks to the west and eases up over the trees.

"Maybe we'll be the first into Customs at Bedwell Harbor," John says as we see only one other boat in Boundary Pass. We slip in and have the dock to ourselves. We are finished in fifteen minutes. "A record," John maneuvers out and we are on our way again.

"There's not a bit of wind," I say, as two sail boats dawdle nearby with their sails up, fooling no one.

The sky is filled with ragged clouds hovering over Vancouver Island. They slowly cluster in gray bubbles leaving us a blue hole above. We cruise along Swanson Channel, a port turn brings us into Captains Passage and we leisurely motor up to Ganges Harbor. A fleet of Canadian boats are on their way out, heading to the next destination.

"Think they're going to the San Juans?" We often meet Canadian boaters in our waters, doing what we are doing in reverse. "Maybe this is our weekend to take the place of a Canadian going to Friday Harbor." I say to John.

"Could be."

We dock in our appointed slip, don our vests and walk toward town. The market at Centennial Park is a favorite place. My friend David will be here with his dragon fly decorated cobalt blue bowls. I'd like to add another to my collection, and find out how his summer has been.

Later, after a simple meal aboard, we will walk the docks in the twilight and watch the moon rise over the boats anchored in the harbor. Then, the gentle creaking of the bow line will lull us into a deep sleep until dawn.

Autumn

Flying

"It's a great day to go flying." John looks at the sky. "How about it?"

I chuck the trowel into the wheelbarrow. "Let me get my sunglasses and cap." We have an RV8 kit plane, the Red Rocket, that John built over the course of three years. I popped a few rivets myself, just to say I had a hand in her birth. John pulls her out of the hangar, she sparkles in the sun and we climb aboard.

In this tandem arrangement I am the GIB (gal in back) with a customized six inch booster seat that allows me to see through the Plexiglas canopy to the wide expanse of sky beyond. We tug our seatbelt straps tight and adjust the radio headsets. Two deer munch on leaves near the hangar door and ignore us as we scoot toward the runway.

We pull off the taxiway for John to complete his checklist. In this slice of time I see my husband as the career pilot he was—focused, serious and efficient. As he turns dials and radios our take-off data he is one with the plane.

The engine roars its readiness and John fastens the canopy. We scream down the runway and climb out high and fast.

In a steep bank that gives me a sweeping view of the west, I admire the great expanse of Vancouver Island. Below, a container ship's wake plows a liquid contrail down Haro Strait. A smattering of yachts and smaller boats give it a wide berth. The Olympic Mountains cast a watchful eye over the Strait of Juan de Fuca.

"When does the beverage service start?" I can't resist the question. I see a half smile cross John's profile. He shakes his head at me.

We float in the air above False Bay and cruise over Cattle Point to inspect Lopez Island. I scan the airspace for other small planes. "Aircraft, eleven o'clock, below us," I speak clearly into the foam covered microphone. I have learned to be a part of this flying team.

We fly in silence for a while, leisurely banking right to see the ferries, left to see boats nosed into their slips in Friday Harbor. We fly higher, zipping through a gauzy shred of white cloud over Mt. Constitution and then Vancouver comes into view.

There isn't any wind today and we cruise with a bird's-eye view of Blakely, Shaw, Waldron, Decatur, Stewart and over the heart of Orcas Island. As we approach Speiden we make a lolling turn toward Roche Harbor Marina and get ready to land. Holding my breath, I listen for the question I have been waiting for.

"Want to go around again?"

"Yes!"

John pushes the throttle forward and the gray ribbon of tarmac disappears beneath us for the second time as we streak over the trees tops in a high climb. Our chores, duties and earth-bound life will have to wait. Today, we fly.

Autumn

Playing in the Rain

"Check your toes for webbing," I take the broom to the pine needles that stubbornly stick to the soles of John's shoes. "What a mess!"

"Not as messy as that," he points to the noon news and the piles of debris on a riverbank on the mainland. "Living on a rock has its advantages." John warms his hands, and then turns his back to the fire in the kitchen fireplace.

Tuxedo looks up as the wind blows a madrona branch past the French doors. He re-arranges his tail across his nose, glances at the fire and sighs.

"My friend Kathryn told me this morning that when she lived on another island it rained so many days in a row the local ducks came into her house through the cat door to get a dose of dry air."

"Another good reason to live on a rock." John drapes his arm across my shoulder. We stand there together listening, to the sizzle and hiss of dry wood burning.

Outside raindrops pelt the window in sheets, and a flurry of pine twigs tumble along the patio. On the lake, geese glide by, impervious to the wet.

Autumn

"After lunch I need to go back to the boat. Want to go?"

"Sure." Any reason to go to the boat is a good one.

When we arrive at the dock, I scrunch my neck deep into my wool sweater and pull my blue scarf up to my nose. The rain plunks a rhythm on my jacket, forms a bead on the brim of my hat and falls in a fat plop on the toe of my scarred boots.

There is no such thing as bad weather I've been told—only inappropriate clothing. More than a grain of truth in that, I think, as I clamber onto the boat. Once aboard, I adjust a fender and tighten a line. I gaze out the big windows as John repairs or replaces the bolt/screw/thing that warranted the trip. The neighboring boat, with a blue sleep mask secured over its pilot house windows, has settled in for the coming rain and wind of winter hibernation.

"All done." John emerges from the engine room and packs away his tools.

"Me, too." I've collected the last food items and towels. Now we can go home, stomp the pine needles off one more time, rub the cat's head until he yowls in protest, and have a steaming cup of hot chocolate.

A pre-hibernation snooze with a purring cat is a method of acclimation to autumn that I enjoy. I see one in my future.

The Ferry Wait

My husband is a native New Yorker. He grew up in Garden City, on the western end of Long Island. His father, upon retirement, spent the last two decades of his life in the old whaling village of Greenport, at the eastern end of the north shore.

In our visits to see Dad, we would stroll down his lane to the water's edge and look out toward Shelter Island, a five minute ferry ride away. In the summer months, on walks into town we skirted cars parked along the street waiting for the ferry. On our return, the same cars with the same sleepy drivers would be in exactly the same spot.

"What's the attraction?" I remember asking John. "I can't imagine anything that would cause me to sit in a car for hours like that."

"It's a choice. They love where they live." John is a sage.

I recounted that conversation to a contingent of Long Islanders at a recent East Coast conference. Many of them, having visited our island, laughed loud and hard.

"Now, I sit for hours to leave San Juan Island and reverse the process to get home." I laugh with them. "Who knew?"

Time and circumstance have a way of changing our perspective. In those earlier days, time was a pie to be sliced into wedges for children, parents, careers and hopefully—a few crumbs for solitude and reflection. To sit idly waiting on a ferry seemed to me a sliver I could ill afford.

These days I realize that the hours I spend in a ferry line are a gift. I recount the books I've read, columns and letters I have written, friends with whom I've talked and the opportunity I've had to simply sit quietly and think. There isn't any waste at all.

At the end of the conference, John and I were invited back to visit Greenport. We thanked our host and agreed that we might just do that.

John mulled this over. "Could be fun to go back to the Sound View Restaurant and go look at the boats."

"Or go to Preston's for a new cookbook." I've warmed to this idea, too. "But I'll have to do one other thing."

"What's that?"

"Go congratulate the folks in one of those cars in the ferry line for choosing to live on an island."

In Praise of November

Yesterday I stood on a hill overlooking Pelindaba Lavender Farm. The acres of lavender bushes, shorn of their fragrant purple displays were at rest—each bush a brown nubby button on the chenille bedspread Mother Nature had tossed over the farm.

At our house the Big Gal has shaken the last of the golden leaves from our river birch tree. The peach and white begonias that bloom near our front door behave like recalcitrant children, stubbornly refusing, in all their wet droopiness, to accept the end of the season. The transplanted vinca, however, has embraced its new location, thriving in the freshly composted bed, snug under a layer of wood chips and digging its way toward well-rootedness.

Last week, my friend Susan and I walked along White Point Road. We passed the apple orchard, its gates wide open in a neighborly welcome. A dozen or so deer nosed around in the piles of bronze and gold leaves. They paused to look at us and then dropped their heads again to feed among the mounds of ruby apples heaped along the row of trees at this feast-of-November event.

At our home, the yard deer have been grazing about, the occasional buck striking a handsome pose on the long rock outside our bedroom window. The spotted fawns of spring now sport brown fur coats and saunter closer when I step outside to chat with them.

Earlier this morning, when the first gust of wind shot a long breath of chilly air into our bedroom, I wondered if the Trumpeter swans would arrive on our lake today. I listened for the familiar honking that comes at daybreak. I heard nothing. I had seen several on Sportsman's Lake on previous trips to town, but I was anxious to see them here, their snowy wings in a graceful arc as they circle the lake and come in for a smooth landing, gliding in and out of sight around Roy Island.

It is a fire-in-the-kitchen-fireplace kind of day and I scuff outside to the porch to get kindling. I scan the lake and stop mid-scuff; a Trumpeter couple ride the lake current just out from our dock. The wind whips my robe around my legs and pine needles hurtle their way toward my fuzzy slippers to meet in a perfect Velcro moment.

I breathe a sigh, somewhere between relief and quiet happiness. This is the snapshot moment that grounds me in the assurance that to everything, there is indeed, a time and a season.

Regardless of the tumult in the world beyond the end of our lane, all is well here, amid the swans and autumnal rains of November.

Second Fiddle

At the beginning of the year, a black and white stray cat showed up at our house. In the howling winds and rain, he moved from under the car, to a box on the porch, an Icelandic blanket in the mudroom, a comfy captain's chair in the kitchen and then staked out an easy chair in the living room.

He did not give up a single spot and re-claims them from time to time as he follows the sun through the seasons.

Initially I called him the handsome stray, then the perpetual guest. At a point when I thought he had selected our home as his more than occasional abode, I formally named him Tuxedo. I have become shamelessly enamored with him, and unfortunately he knows it.

Tonight, as I sat on the sofa wondering what the heck I was going to write about, he wandered in through his private door, picked up a bit of catnip and shook it twice, then strolled over to the sofa where he nodded to John and mewed instructions at me.

Ever the obedient staffer, I followed him to his dish in the kitchen, refilled it and freshened his water. As he cleaned the bowl, I returned to the sofa, smoothed a blanket over my lap and waited. If the stars were aligned in a proper order he might deign to sit between us.

They were not. Once again I was the object on the sofa he jumped over on his way to the blue-jeaned lap of the man that was reading a book, not at all interested in a black-and-white mobile heater that thumped his head on the man's chin and insisted on unencumbered lap time.

I watched the slow man-dance between Tuxedo and John. They spoke in grunts and head butted each other. I wouldn't have been surprised had Tuxedo lifted his paw in a high five. John pretended to be uninterested and the cat adored him.

I, on the other hand, begged, implored, cajoled, wheedled, whined, sniffled and offered my lap and the promise of still more food cooked to perfection in a solid copper pan, infused with essence of wild salmon—all to no avail.

With a deep sigh I eventually came to the inevitable conclusion that this was not a failure on my part. I have simply perfected the art of second fiddle.

Autumn

Winter

Winter

Lost and Found

Heidi sat me down in her kitchen last Saturday—with eggnog latte with extra nutmeg—and fell into the telling of this story.

A fiery opal crown surrounded by diamonds adorned a stickpin of great historical importance to her. It's presence on her lapel brought a sense of comfort, a tangible connection to her past. While she and her husband Jack were shopping, several clerks and proprietors had mentioned its beauty, style and timelessness.

On their return from town she glanced down to find it gone. According to Jack, the primeval sounds she emitted rivaled those, he felt sure, of a dying primate.

She was in the truck before he could utter a word. "We must go back now."

In town, Heidi retraced her steps. Each shopkeeper heard her tale of woe and many joined her in the careful inspection of floors, doorjambs and sidewalks.

In the drugstore, Jack painstakingly searched the aisles on his hands and knees to no avail. He left the store to see forty or so people, fanned out across the street and sidewalk in the hunt for the opal crown stickpin. There were elderly folk, young people, a child on a bike—all focused in the search for this irreplaceable piece of Heidi's past.

With no trace of the pin, a heavy hearted duo returned home, devastated. But Heidi could not rest. The pin had to be somewhere. People had noticed it in town, so what had she done on their return home? They had stopped and picked up the mail. Then what? She had thrown the trash mail into a re-cycle bin. Of course! Maybe, just maybe, yes, there it was, winking away, waiting patiently to be found.

Heidi opened her hand and showed me the pin. "Here, it is." I stayed to hear the great unraveling of the story of how her grandmother came to have it, and I watched the parade of emotions march across Heidi's face in the telling. I began to understand why its loss would have rendered her inconsolable.

"I've got to let the people who helped me look know that I've found it." She reached for a tissue. "Write a letter, do something." She handed me the tissue box. "All those people stopped and looked and they need to be thanked."

"This is why we live here." We spoke simultaneously.

And so, this is a column about loss, hope, and exultation— a seasonal reminder with tidings of comfort and joy.

The Last Straw

Last evening I spent a few minutes re-reading a wonderful children's story, *The Last Straw* written by Fredrick H. Thury. I open it every year and give myself a great mid-December boost.

Hoshmakaka is an old camel called upon to carry gifts to a baby king in Bethlehem. He responds with a reluctance that's understandable. "My gout," he cries, "my joints, my sciatica." He has another commitment, a cud-chewing convention in Beemish it seems.

Grudgingly he agrees to make the trip, bragging about his stamina and strength. He finds the journey filled with many people ready to add one more gift to the ever growing pile on his back. He knows he's not as strong as he says, but he accommodates the weight of the gifts until, as the title implies, one more thing will send him to his bony knees.

The month of December can make me feel Hoshmakaka'd. There is always one more volunteer request that I should add to the pile on my back, one more errand, one last package, one last card to mail.

I mumble under my breath that I don't have time; it's too

cold, I'm too hot, and my plans for the month are quickly falling into the crack of life between later and never. Then I stop and get a grip on myself. I am blessed to have a life without want, to be warm, to have family and friends with whom I can share good times and who will help me through my dark hours.

Old Hoshmakaka arrived in Bethlehem and completed his mission. He delivered his gifts to the baby king, including the gift of one last straw. The book doesn't say, but I think he returned to the oasis, rubbed ointment on his knees, and made plans to win the water-drinking contest in Rangal later in the month.

Let's see, today is December 12th. There is still time to make a wreath, cook a meal, donate some firewood to the friend of a friend and a basket of food to the food bank. There is time to reflect on the sacredness of the season, have a cup of tea and a walk with a neighbor.

I've taken the Hoshmakaka test this morning. I've stretched my back, tested my joints, and flexed my knees. I'm a long way from the last straw.

Sights and Lights

"December is my favorite time of the year in London." I tucked my hand into granddaughter Rachel's pocket as we headed to a bakery shop for a morning coffee. "Thank you for asking me to come and share this with you." I had arrived at her flat in Earl's Court for a week's visit.

"I'm so glad you're here to see me." She squeezed my hand impatiently. "I've mapped out a possible itinerary." She handed it to me for a look-over. "What do you think?"

I looked up at a partly cloudy sky. "If the weather will cooperate." The weather, with the exception of one night of light showers did remain uncommonly clear and cold.

We spent our days perusing our favorite museums, caught a show—*The Thirty-Nine Steps* at the Criterion Theatre. We were privileged to get an individual tour of Parliament by a friend of Rachel's, an aide to a member of the House of Lords. I tucked my pass for that event away. The sun added a memory of its own—a shaft of glittering light on Big Ben.

On another afternoon, Rach looked at our "to-see" list.

"There's a German Christmas Market on the South Bank. After tea, of course."

"Perfect. I need an ornament for a friend." I snugged my scarf tight around my neck. "Let's go."

We took the Tube to Westminster, and strolled across Westminster Bridge—slowed by a whiff of roasting chestnuts—to the South Bank of the Thames. A light mist was falling as we walked past the London Eye, the modern Ferris wheel that provides a bird's eye view of the city. It has most assuredly redefined the London skyline.

Rachel pointed up. "Remember our ride on that?"

"What a view, but it's too close to the Abbey."

"Oh, Grandma." Rachel propelled me forward to sound and light. "Things change."

The vendors from Cologne, Germany had set up shop in kiosks along the river. Each one was a bright square of light in the deepening twilight. A large carousel of ponies carried squealing young children on an undulating ride away from their parents and then safely back again.

Farther along, the ginger-bready smells of Lebkuchen made my nose twitch, but I will-powered my way past. I was there for an ornament and found a small wooden Christmas tree from the Schwarzwald, or Black Forest region. Susan will be pleased.

Later in the week we attended the Evensong service at Westminster Abbey. I slipped the program into my pocket. This too I will keep. For as many years as I have gone to London, evensong at Westminster remains my favorite thing. The sun shone that day, and the faultless voices of the choir of the Abbey soared high into the arches, drawing my eyes to the stained glass window above me. The powerful sounds of the organ swaddled the words of the ageless hymn and lingered over the last amen.

There were other delights in our forays across the city. There was the lighting of the Norwegian Spruce Christmas Tree in Trafalgar Square, the giant stars of tiny lights spider-webbed across Regent Street. More quickly than I wished my week with Rachel ended.

I thought about all that I had seen as the ferry bumped its way into the dock on my arrival home. None of it compared to the tree in Memorial Park that welcomed me with its strand of lights, the 'Noel' sign above the Front Street Ale House, and the lights along Spring Street and in the windows of the shops and businesses of folks I know. The white snowflakes hanging from the street light poles guided me down Second Street as I headed out of town and into darkness. I searched for the familiar lights from homes tucked back into the evergreens and smiled at the simple glowing outline of the chapel at San Juan Vineyard as I passed it by.

These are the sights that comfort me, for these are the lights that lead me home.

Winter

Seven Swans a Swimming

Christmas Day is almost over and I've got my new blue robe, my fire-engine red slippers and several books that I can savor slowly over the weeks to come. One includes the *Best American Names of Horses Expected to Have Undistinguished Careers* by Mike Richardson-Bryant. As a writer this could be an important list when talking to friends from Louisville, Kentucky. My favorite name from that list is *For the Love of God Run Faster*, followed by *Glued Lightning*. To counterbalance such frivolity, I received two historical books on WWII that give me somber pause.

Mother Nature brought her gifts too. They are ones I have come to expect but have never taken for granted. In November three Trumpeter swans unpacked their goose down travelling bags on the banks of the lake, fanned their feathers and readied themselves for a winter stay. Those three seemed to enjoy Heidi and Jack's secluded coves and rarely ventured our way.

"I hope that's not all we have," I said to John one December morning.

"They'll be along." John said.

I thought about that as I slipped into bed at the end of Christmas day. On Christmas Eve eve, two elegant swans— no, make that three, four, five, six, seven elegant swans—had glided to a stop to feed just beneath the patio. The chosen sentry had floated in guard duty mode, watching the shore-line carefully. The others had tilted their-oh-so-sparkling-white bottoms skyward as they fed.

The swans had enjoyed themselves as an apple pie turned brown in the oven and a turkey pouted in the thawing pan. A throng of resident ducks had paddled by and said hello on their way to Roy Island. Two bald eagles had called to each other in the trees.

Like the small thoughtful gifts from my family, the swans arrive each year faithfully and without fanfare. I anticipate and am delighted in their arrival.

I plump my pillow to perfection, stretch out beneath a just-the-right-weight comforter and wiggle my toes in the land of fleece and flannel. I am in a state of contented weariness. "We have a great life, babe."

John sighs deeply and reaches for the lamp switch. "We do."

"I'm happy. You?" I listen for an affirmation.

It comes—seconds later—in the sounds of deep relaxed breathing.

I smile at the stars through the skylight and count swans on my way to sleep.

Mary Walley Kalbert is a columnist for IslandGuardian.com. She lives in San Juan County, Washington with her husband John, and the occasional cat. She is a native daughter of Greene County, Mississippi.

Future works may be found at www.marykalbert.com

To order copies of this book, contact Mary at marykalbert@ marykalbert.com.